CHEF ROB GAYLE'S
FAVORITE
CARIBBEAN
DELIGHTS

This has been a beautiful journey!
First of course I have to thank God, my mother...the real momma chef and my sister Jackie, (Precious), for inspiring her little big brother. I want to thank the Matthews Seafood Restaurant, (Ocean Beach, Fire Island), for giving me my start. The Culinary Institute of America for putting the structure in place.

I have to also acknowledge all of the restaurants that allowed me to be creative; G.D. Grafitti in Woodbury Commons, Long Island and Rigatoni's in Rockville Centre, Long Island. Most of all Sean "P. Diddy" Combs for giving me the opportunity and trusting me to embark on the expansion of his Justin's Restaurant brand to Atlanta, Georgia in 1998.

A very special thank you to my wife Tashauna, Roan, Lisa, Byron, Sharika, Courtney, Shakeya, and the Gayle family for their unwavering support of my vision.

To my very loyal customers for their support, feedback, and constructive criticism along the way; I thank you and hope you continue to enjoy Chef Rob's Caribbean Cafe, Upscale Lounge, and Food Truck.

ISBN: 978-1-6653-0463-4
eISBN: 978-1-6653-0464-1

Copyright 2022 by Robert Gayle

All rights reserved. No part of this book may be reproduced or utilized in any form or by any means, electronic or mechanical, including photocopying, recording, or by any information storage or retrieval system, without permission in writing from the author.

TABLE OF CONTENTS

RECIPES

Jerk Chicken Egg Rolls	1
Shrimp Skewers	3
Double Crab Cakes	5
Jerk Chicken Wings	7
BBQ Spare Ribs	9
Whole Red Snapper (Escovitch)	11
Blackened Mango Chicken	13
Blackened North Atlantic Salmon	15
Chef Rob's White Chocolate Bread Pudding with Bailey's Cream Sauce	17

JERK CHICKEN EGG ROLLS

INGREDIENTS:

- 3 oz. diced chicken breast (jerked)
- 3 oz. julienne cut zucchini, yellow squash, carrots, cabbage
- Egg roll skins

MANGO MARMALADE INGREDIENTS:

- 8 oz. mango chutney
- 4 oz. orange juice
- 1 tbs. of ginger
- 1 oz. scallion (chopped)
- 2 oz. of brown sugar

COOKING INSTRUCTIONS:

1. Sauté vegetables in a skillet with light butter. Add salt & white pepper.
2. Mix diced jerk chicken breast with sautéed vegetables.
3. Roll up ingredients into the egg roll skins.
4. Deep fry the egg rolls for 2 minutes at 325 degrees.
5. For decoration, drizzle plate with mango marmalade.

MARMALADE COOKING INSTRUCTIONS:

Cook all ingredients together on medium temperature in a sauce pan.
Puree with blender to obtain texture.

SHRIMP SKEWERS

INGREDIENTS:

- 9 shrimp (3 shrimp per skewer)

PINA COLADA SAUCE
INGREDIENTS & PREPARATION:

- 1 cup pina colada mix
- ½ cup pineapple juice
- 1 cup sweet chilli

Mix ingredients together and sauce is complete.

COOKING INSTRUCTIONS:

1. Sauté lightly in oil until nice and brown.
2. Get rid of excess grease.
3. Add pina colada sauce on top and let simmer.
4. Place in center core of grilled pineapple.

DOUBLE CRAB CAKES

INGREDIENTS:

- *1lb real crab meat*
- *1 beaten egg*
- *2 tbs mayo*
- *1 tbs dry mustard*
- *1 tsp seasoning salt*
- *½ tsp of lemon juice*
- *¾ cup of bread crumbs*
- *1 tsp of chopped parsley*

COOKING INSTRUCTIONS:

1. Mix all ingredients together & form your patties.
2. Sear in butter & oil mix on medium heat for 1 minute on each side until nice and brown.
3. Garnish with a sprig of parsley.

JERK CHICKEN WINGS

INGREDIENTS:

- *1 & 2'S (Flat and drum)*
- *¼ cup oil*
- *1 Tbs cumin*
- *1 cup jerk seasoning*
- *4 oz. of oyster sauce*
- *2 Tbs seasoning salt*

COOKING INSTRUCTIONS:

1. Mix oil, cumin, jerk seasoning, salt & oyster sauce together.
2. Marinate wings and allow to soak over night.
3. Grill or bake wings until golden brown and thoroughly cooked.

BBQ RIBS

INGREDIENTS:

- *2 cups sugar*
- *4 oz. cayenne*
- *4 oz. chilli*
- *8 oz. paprika*
- *4 oz. cumin*
- *4 oz. black pepper*
- *1 cup kosher*

COOKING INSTRUCTIONS:

1. Mix all ingredients together and add dry rub over the ribs.
2. Allow to marinate overnight.
3. Put in the oven with enough water to cover the ribs. Cover.
4. Cook for 3 hours at 300°.

WHOLE RED SNAPPER (ESCOVITCH)

PREPARATION:

- Clean, gut and scale Fish
- Season lightly with salt & pepper
- Add 1 tablespoon Garlic
- Add 2 tsp of Oil

ESCOVITCH SAUCE INGREDIENTS:

- ½ oil
- 2 red peppers
- 2 green peppers
- 2 onions
- 2 scotch bonnet peppers
- 20 pimento seeds
- 3 oz. fresh thyme
- 1 can whole tomato
- ½ can ketchup
- 3 cups vinegar
- ½ cup sugar
- ½ cup chicken stock
- 2 Bay Leaves

COOKING INSTRUCTIONS:

1. Place whole fish in Fryer.
2. Assure fish is cooked completely.
3. Place fish in saute pan.
4. Add Escovitch sauce, fresh thyme, and a pat of butter.
5. Reduce sauce.

ESCOVITCH SAUCE COOKING INSTRUCTIONS:

1. Sauté all vegetables in oil.
2. Add tomato product, vinegar, and sugar.
3. Add fresh thyme.
4. Add all ingredients, then simmer for 10 minutes.

BLACKENED MANGO CHICKEN W/ COCONUT RICE & PLANTAINS

INGREDIENTS:

- (2) 6 oz. chicken breasts

COCONUT RICE INGREDIENTS:

- 6 oz. cooked Jasmine rice
- 2 oz. coconut milk
- salt & pepper to taste
- fresh chopped parsley
- Finely minced scotch bonett pepper
- (optional)
- 1 oz. whole butter

MANGO SALSA INGREDIENTS:

- 1 fresh mango (peeled & julienne cut)
- ½ green pepper
- ½ red pepper
- ½ onion
- 2 oz. lime juice
- salt & pepper (to taste)
- fresh cilantro
- 1 oz. oil
- 2 oz. sugar

COOKING INSTRUCTIONS:

1. Sprinkle blackening seasoning over (2) 6 oz. chicken breast.
2. Sear it on very hot sautee pan, make sure you achieve 165 degreees internal temperature.

COCONUT RICE PREPARATION:

Add rice in bowl with all ingredients and mix well

MANGO SALSA PREPARATION:

1. Mix it all ingredients together & heat salsa over medium temperature
2. Add mango salsa over prepared chicken

PLANTAINS PREPARATION:

Pan or deep fry 3 peeled plantains until they have a nice brown color.

BLACKENED SALMON

**SERVING OPTIONS:
GRILLED, BBQ, POACHED, BLACKENED**

All Served with Jasmine Rice and Collard Greens

INGREDIENTS:

- *1 Serving Steak-cut bone-in*
- *North Atlantic salmon*
  *bone-in adds more flavor
- *8 oz chicken stock*
- *1 oz chopped garlic*
- *2 sprigs of fresh thyme*
- *2 pats of butter*
- *1 bay leaf*
- *Pinch of saffron (optional)*

COOKING INSTRUCTIONS:

1. Add chicken stock, garlic, thyme, butter, and bay leaf to pot to create poaching liquid.
2. Let mixture come to a boil
3. Add salmon and simmer for 10 minutes
4. Let steam until fully cooked

WHITE CHOCOLATE BREAD PUDDING

YIELD: 1 FULL HOTEL PAN = 21 PIECES

INGREDIENTS:

- *3 each french baguette or sour*
- *1 quart heavy cream*
- *1 quart half and half cream*
- *1- 12oz. package of white*
- *chocolate morsel*
- *¼ pint can of condensed milk*
- *2 cup sugar*
- *4oz. vanilla*
- *4 eggs*
- *6 oz. Bailey's liquor*

PREPARATION:

Cut bread into 1" cubes
Place in buttered pan

COOKING INSTRUCTIONS:

1. Heat cream with sugar and vanilla until hot.
- [NOTE] BE CAREFUL NOT TO SCORCH
2. Remove from heat.
3. Add condense milk.
4. Add white chocolate. Let cool.
5. Add beaten eggs.
6. Pour over cubed bread in pan.
7. Allow to soak for 30 minutes.
8. Spray top with butter spray.
9. Cover with parchment paper.
10. Cover tightly with aluminum paper.

11. Place in oven at 300 for 1 hour.
12. Take off aluminum paper and let top brown for 10 minutes.
13. Place on rack and allow to cool.

After cooling cut the bread pudding into 21 even rectangular pieces.

ChefRob's
CARIBBEAN CAFE
Cooking Classes

VISIT
CHEFROBS.EVENTBRITE.COM
TO RSVP FOR THE NEXT COOKING CLASS DATE!

About Chef Rob

Robert Gayle, the Executive Chef and Owner at Chef Rob's Caribbean Cafe & Upscale Lounge, combines his Caribbean background with his own culinary sophistication, to gather flavors from around the world for a refined menu of island comfort fare. Known for his unique approach to bringing fresh ideas to old favorites, while also creating signature dishes, Chef Rob's mental rolodex includes recipes for top-selling entrees such as braised beef oxtails, ackee and salt fish, jerk chicken, curried goat, dry-rubbed spare ribs, and his illustrious spicy jerk seasoning.

Chef Rob's history is as distinctive as his food. After spending his childhood in Jamaica West Indies, Chef Rob relocated to the United States. At the age of 13, good food began to make a lasting impression on him as his culinary love developed while working as a steward on Fire Island, New York. After obtaining his degree from the Culinary Institute of America in 1993, Chef Rob's skills and prestige steadily increased, allowing him to assist with the openings of Sean 'P. Diddy' Combs' New York and Atlanta venture, Justin's Restaurant, in 1997. The momentum has since continued with Chef Rob's own ventures and celebrities including Usher, Shaquille O'Neal, Wale, T-Pain, Sheree Whitfield, Bobby Valentino, and more have been spotted visiting his venue.

In 2013 Atlanta Mayor Kasim Reed penned a congratulatory letter to Chef Rob for the opening of his upscale lounge. Chef Rob was also voted 'fan favorite' at the 2013 Atlanta Chef's Expo, and selected by Uptown Magazine as the featured Atlanta Chef for their "Discover Artful Infusions" series. He makes it a priority to participate in various community events, and since 2013 has served an annual Caribbean Thanksgiving Dinner for families in need at the Mary Hall Freedom House. Chef Rob has been featured in Hype Magazine (2014), Who's Who of Black Atlanta (2014) and in 2016, he had the privilege of catering for Jonetta Patton's Culinary Incubator. Chef Rob became the Winner of the Second Annual "Food that Rocks" event hosted by Taste of Atlanta, while also receiving a glowing review by Atlanta Eats in 2017.

After nearly 10 successful years as a restauranteur, Chef Rob's ability to surprise and innovate continues to evolve as his passion for making and sharing the best of Caribbean Cuisine with anyone who loves to eat is embodied in his great-tasting food. The Chef Rob brand has expanded to include a new Caribbean food truck, specialty sauces, intimate cooking classes, and event catering options. Chef Rob is proud to serve the Greater Atlanta area and on any given day, he can be found doing what he loves best – putting smiles on the faces of those enjoying his scrumptious culinary creations

www.ingramcontent.com/pod-product-compliance
Lightning Source LLC
Chambersburg PA
CBHW061213070526
44583CB00025B/3228